SHIPS
THROUGH TIME

ROY RICHARDS

MACDONALD YOUNG BOOKS

First published in 1995 by Macdonald Young Books Ltd

Text © Roy Richards 1995
Illustration © Macdonald Young Books Ltd 1995

Macdonald Young Books Ltd
Campus 400
Maylands Avenue
Hemel Hempstead
Herts HP2 7EZ

Illustrator: Ross Watton, The Garden Studio
Designer: Celia Hart
Commissioning editor: Debbie Fox
Editor: Jayne Booth
Consultants: Simon Stephens and
Alec Fearon C. Eng, Eur. Ing.

We are grateful to the following for permission to reproduce photographs: Robert Harding (p. 16); Michael Holford (pp. 8, 12); London Science Museum (p. 28); The Master and Fellows Magdalene College, Cambridge (p. 20); National Maritime Museum (p. 24).

The Publishers would like to thank the following for their help: Kathy Baxendale; Alison Couper (Sea Containers); Bob Cripps, Gill Mace, Georgette Purches, Lisa Symes (RNLI); Eila Henderson (Lloyds Register); Hoverspeed; Keith Johnson; Emma Parkin (British Marine Industries Federation); Port of London Authority; Brian Rees (Stena Sealink Line); Dr Margaret Rule (Mary Rose Trust); Mark Rymell; Nigel Weare (Amateur Rowing Association).

Printed and bound in Hong Kong by the Paramount Printing Group.

ISBN 0 7500 1333 8

CONTENTS

THE FIRST BOATS

EGYPTIAN PAPYRUS BOAT
Papyrus reeds were a plentiful resource along the River Nile. The ancient Egyptians bundled them together to make boats.

Humans have travelled by water for thousands of years. Moving on the water was easier and quicker than over land, and boats could also transport large cargoes over great distances. Through the ages, different materials have been used to make boats depending on what was available and how clever people were at building them. When people first travelled by water they probably used a floating tree trunk. Then they learned to tie logs together or use other materials like bundled reeds to make rafts. Animal skins were used to make floats or to cover a framework of bamboo or willow to make a watertight boat. Some of these materials are still used today.

THE KON-TIKI

The *Kon-Tiki* was built by explorer Thor Heyerdahl. He wanted to prove such a raft could cross the Pacific Ocean. *Kon-Tiki* was a copy of an ancient South American raft and was made of long balsa wood logs. They were bound together with about 300 pieces of rope – no nails were used at all. A short thick log across the back supported the steering oar and two strong posts held the sail. The voyage took place in 1947 with six men on board. It lasted 95 days and was a success.

roof made of
banana leaves

cabin made
of bamboo

bamboo
deck

side logs
9 metres long

steering oar

central logs
14 metres long

wooden pegs

tie with string

lolly sticks

A MODEL RAFT

A simple but effective raft can be made from clothes pegs. Either jam them onto lolly sticks or tie them with string. Use the waterproof type of card from a milk carton to make a cabin.

use the card from a milk carton to make a cabin

LAKE TITICACA

Lake Titicaca is so high in the Andes (3,500 metres above sea level) that wood is scarce. But reeds grow around the lake and have been used to build boats for many centuries.

Ghengis Khan, the Mongol conqueror, used goat skins blown up like balloons as floats. This way his army crossed the great River Oxus in Central Asia.

inflated animal skins float

The prehistoric coracle is still used today on rivers in Wales and south-west England. The coracler paddles with the stream to move sideways across the river.

one-person coracles are light enough to carry

North American Inuit use kayaks for hunting because they move very quickly. Kayaks are made of light driftwood frames with sealskins sewn together and stretched over them.

some Inuit now use painted canvas to cover kayaks

KEEPING DRY

The Inuit people developed the kayak – a type of canoe with a covered top. The top helped to prevent the boat being swamped in rough water and kept the paddler dry. The Inuit wore animal skins to keep them warm and dry and even laced their clothes into the skin covering the kayak to keep the boat watertight. Today, paddlers wear wet-suits and spray/splash decks – a sort of apron which then seals the top of the kayak.

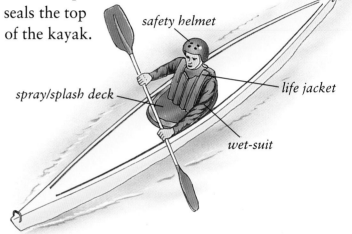

safety helmet

spray/splash deck

life jacket

wet-suit

PADDLING

Paddling is a way of moving and steering a boat through the water using body strength. The first paddles were probably just branches, but today the most modern kayak paddles are made of Kevlar carbon fibre – the same material used to build Formula 1 racing cars. The paddler puts the blade of the paddle in front and pulls the boat through the water.

Single paddles are used in open-top canoes. Twisting the paddle in the water or pulling harder on one side also steers the canoe.

Double paddles are used in kayaks. The blades are set at an angle to each other so there is less air resistance on the blade out of the water.

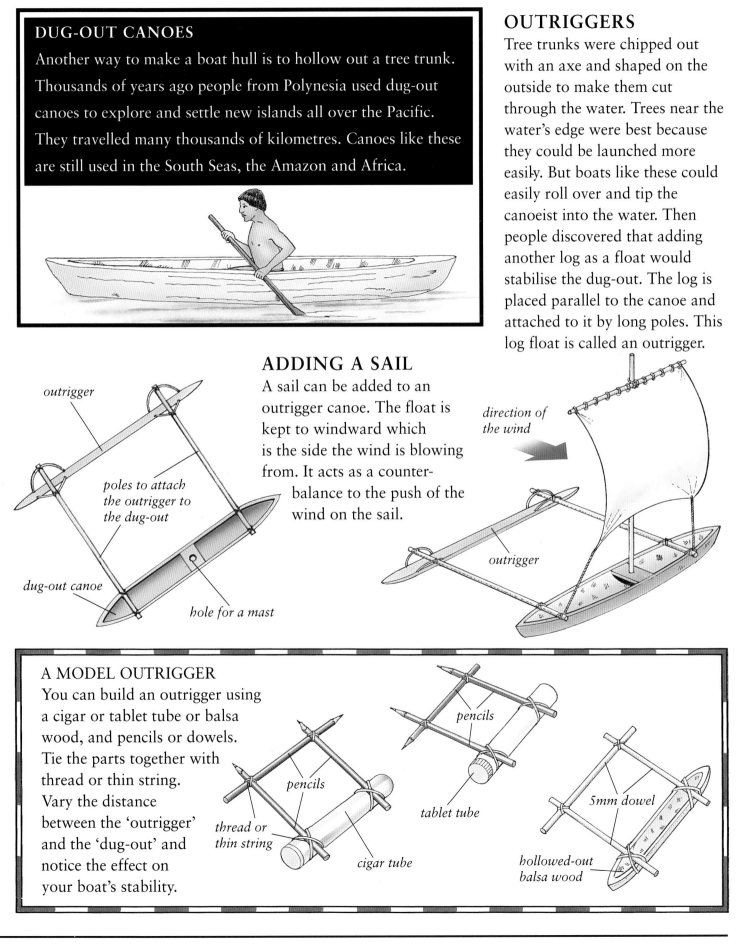

DUG-OUT CANOES

Another way to make a boat hull is to hollow out a tree trunk. Thousands of years ago people from Polynesia used dug-out canoes to explore and settle new islands all over the Pacific. They travelled many thousands of kilometres. Canoes like these are still used in the South Seas, the Amazon and Africa.

OUTRIGGERS

Tree trunks were chipped out with an axe and shaped on the outside to make them cut through the water. Trees near the water's edge were best because they could be launched more easily. But boats like these could easily roll over and tip the canoeist into the water. Then people discovered that adding another log as a float would stabilise the dug-out. The log is placed parallel to the canoe and attached to it by long poles. This log float is called an outrigger.

ADDING A SAIL

A sail can be added to an outrigger canoe. The float is kept to windward which is the side the wind is blowing from. It acts as a counter-balance to the push of the wind on the sail.

outrigger

poles to attach the outrigger to the dug-out

dug-out canoe

hole for a mast

direction of the wind

outrigger

A MODEL OUTRIGGER

You can build an outrigger using a cigar or tablet tube or balsa wood, and pencils or dowels. Tie the parts together with thread or thin string. Vary the distance between the 'outrigger' and the 'dug-out' and notice the effect on your boat's stability.

pencils

thread or thin string

pencils

cigar tube

tablet tube

5mm dowel

hollowed-out balsa wood

ANCIENT GALLEYS

The Roman galleys above are a carving on Trajan's Column, which was built in AD114 to record Rome's victory over the Dacians in AD101–106. Here you can see the Roman rowers using oar power.

Paddling was probably the first method people used to propel their boats. The next advance was rowing where people discovered that by facing the back of the boat and pulling a long oar through the water they were using their body strength more efficiently. The oar had to be pivoted on the side of the boat and this way longer oars could be used and bigger boats could be propelled. But rowing created a new problem – how to steer the boat – and so steering oars and then rudders were developed as ways of directing ships. The ancient Greeks and Romans built large fighting ships with many rowers on board, as the illustration of a Roman war galley shows.

THE GREEK TRIREME

Greek triremes also had a large pointed battering ram at the front for sinking ships. They could move very rapidly – up to 8 knots – and their speed gave great force to the ram.

in a bireme, there were two tiers of oars – about 120 men

biremes were about 24 metres long and 3 metres wide

in a trireme, there were three tiers of oars – about 170 men

triremes were about 43 metres long and 5 metres wide

PUSHING WITH 'OARS'

Fill a washing-up bowl with water. Use a wooden spoon as an oar. With the bowl of the spoon just below the surface of the water, push your 'oar' through the water from back to front. Try it with a short oar and then with a long oar. Now paddle with your spoon by moving it from front to back. Which is the easiest way to move the water?

short oar

long oar

A ROMAN MERCHANT SHIP

The Romans had a huge empire. They brought goods over great distances to supply Rome and they traded with many other nations. To carry their cargoes, they developed merchant ships. They could set the sails to steer the ship as well as move it. Two large oars at the stern were used to improve the steering.

RUDDERS

The rudder was invented by the Chinese over 5,000 years ago and it is still used today. It is a flat piece of wood or metal hinged to the back of a vessel and it stands upright in the water. The rudder works by pushing against the flow of water passing along the hull, which causes the ship to change direction. This is one of the easiest ways of steering a moving ship. Rudders have great force because they are deep in the water and have more surface area than steering oars, so they are strong enough to steer large ships too.

Large rowing boats have rudders to help when steering. Some have ropes attached to them. By pulling the ropes, the person sitting at the back of the boat can steer.

steering ropes

rudder

THE DEVELOPMENT OF STEERING

Early travel by water was probably in small boats which floated with the currents in the water. As boats became larger and people wanted to travel against the wind or currents, they had to invent ways of steering. Although the rudder was invented 5,000 years ago, it wasn't used in the West until the twelfth century.

Early boats could be pushed along and steered using a long pole. People still do this today – it is called punting.

You can steer using a paddle by pulling harder on one side of the boat.

Over 4,500 years ago the Egyptians were among the first to steer their boats using two large steering oars at the stern.

TILLERS

Another device for moving a rudder is a tiller. This is a horizontal bar attached to the top of the rudder. The tiller is kept parallel with the boat to make it travel straight ahead. Turning the tiller to the right moves the rudder to the left causing the water to push against it and turning the boat to the left.

The opposite happens if the tiller is turned to the left.

hook   elastic band   bead

pin

propeller

cardboard rudder

small metal bracket

shaped balsa wood raft

AIR-SCREW BOAT

Make an air-screw boat using the materials shown in the diagram. Wind the elastic band and try it out with the rudder straight. The boat should move in a straight line. Bend the rudder to the right. Which way does the boat go – right or left?

rudder straight

rudder bent to the right

direction water is pushed

The Chinese invented rudders. They controlled the rudder with a tiller.

As ships became larger, mechanical help was needed to move the tiller and rudder.

Until the early eighteenth century, the whipstaff was used to move the tiller. It was difficult to control in rough seas.

Then the wheel was developed in the early eighteenth century. Turning the wheel pulled ropes attached to the tiller which then controlled the rudder. This is an easier way to control the tiller than the whipstaff.

whipstaff

tiller

rudder

wheel

ropes and pulleys

tiller

THE VIKING SHIP

Figureheads were often carved on the bow in the shape of snakes or dragons.

The Vikings from Scandinavia are famed for their seamanship. Their ships were strong and well designed to withstand rough seas as well as travelling up rivers. The shape of the bow of the ships helped them to cut through the water while the flatter bottom gave them stability. The ships could be rowed, but the Vikings also used large square sails mounted on strong oak masts. Between AD 800 and 1070 the Vikings dominated the seas of north Europe, reaching the Mediterranean, and even crossing the Atlantic Ocean to Iceland, Greenland and North America.

A SHALLOW DRAUGHT

The Viking ships were built of planks using the 'clinker' method. This means each plank overlapped the one beneath it. Any gaps between the planks were filled, or caulked, with animal hair soaked in tar. Using these methods, the Vikings could make a hull of any size watertight. Warships were narrow and shallow so that they could make their way up rivers and estuaries easily and be beached safely. Merchant ships for carrying cargoes were also shallow but broader.

yard

T-shaped upright

STOWING THE SAIL

When rowing ashore, the sail and the yard were laid along T-shaped uprights. This gave more deck space and the ship was easier to control and more stable because the sail's weight was over the centre line.

MAKE A SAILING SHIP

You can make your own Viking ship. Carefully cut out the hull from balsa wood. You can use a cocktail stick for the mast. Cut out a square sail from paper and attach it to the mast. Now launch your ship in a bowl of water and blow at it from different directions to see how the sail catches the wind.

shape a hull from balsa wood

pierce a paper sail with a cocktail stick

attach the sail and mast to the hull

LACK OF WIND

We know that the Vikings had different types of ships – some for trade and others for war. The ships' sails were made of panels of homespun wool which were sewn together. If there was no wind or if a battle was to be fought, the Vikings could row their ships. They put their oars through wooden ports and sometimes lowered the mast and sail. There were no fixed rowing benches and each sailor probably sat on his sea chest.

SAILING BEFORE THE WIND

It was easier to sail a Viking ship when the wind was behind it. If the wind was too far round to the side it would have rolled the ship over. This was because Viking ships didn't have a deep keel (see opposite).

The Vikings probably used ropes to hold the sail to catch the wind, although we have no archaeological evidence for this.

DEVELOPMENT OF THE SAIL

Many types of sail have been used through the ages. Here are some different sail arrangements. Sailing ships have to adjust the size of the sails to suit the strength of the wind. If the wind is very strong the sail size must be reduced. This is called 'reefing'.

2500 BC
The Egyptian trader had a square sail. In storms the size of the sail had to be reduced by lowering the yard. This was an early method of reefing.

yard

MIDDLE AGES TO TODAY
Chinese junk sails were made in sections so they could be rolled up and down according to the wind strength.

bamboo battens

SAILING CLOSE TO THE WIND

No sailing ship can sail directly into the wind, but some can sail 'closer' or more towards it than others. Modern yachts with a deep keel can set their sails so that they move forwards at a sharp angle towards the wind. This is called beating. They can also go forwards with the wind blowing across their sides. This is called reaching.

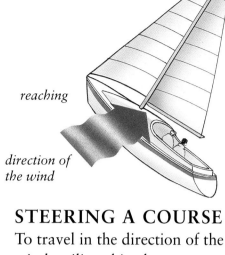

reaching

direction of the wind

direction of the wind

beating

STEERING A COURSE

To travel in the direction of the wind, sailing ships have to follow a zig-zag course by beating one way into the wind and then turning and beating the other way. This method is called tacking.

ADDING A KEEL

A keel helps to prevent a sailing ship from being pushed over on its side by the force of the wind on the sails. Make a keel for your Viking ship by fixing a nail to the bottom. Does it make your ship more stable?

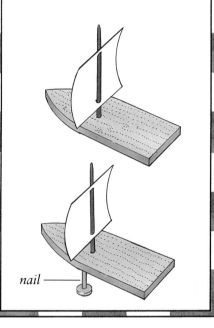

nail

NINETEENTH CENTURY
This square-rigged ship could adjust the size of its sails and the angle at which they were set to get the best use of the wind.

TODAY
On a modern yacht, the front edge of the main sail is attached to the mast making it rigid. This means it can sail 'closer' into the direction of the wind.

main sail

keel

THE FIRST WARSHIP

THE MARY ROSE
The Mary Rose *was built in 1510 and reconstructed in 1534. She sank in 1545 and was not found until 1967. She was finally raised to the surface in 1982.*

The Tudor Kings, Henry VII and Henry VIII, designed the first warships, which led to England's dominance at sea during the sixteenth century. These ships had strong hulls and decks which could take the weight of heavy guns. But heavy guns had to be put in lower decks to maintain the ship's stability. This meant holes, called ports, had to be cut low in the hull for the guns to point through, but they also had to shut to stay watertight. The need for gun ports led to a new way of building hulls. Instead of 'clinker' planking (see page 16) where the planks overlap each other, the Tudors used 'carvel' planking where they were fixed edge to edge. In July 1545, the *Mary Rose* was ready for battle against the French in Portsmouth Harbour. She was very heavy. As she turned, she tilted over and, because her hull was low in the water and her gun ports were open, the sea rushed in. This made her tilt even more until she capsized and quickly sank.

ARMAMENTS

Until the sixteenth century, sea battles were won by boarding the enemy's ships. With guns, a navy could sink enemy ships from a distance. The *Mary Rose* had 91 guns made of bronze or iron. When she was rebuilt in 1534, heavier guns were fitted, adding to her weight. Of her crew of 700 men, 285 were heavily armed soldiers.

The Mary Rose *carried this type of cannon. It was bronze, 3.3 metres long and weighed 2 tonnes.*

SEAWORTHINESS

To be seaworthy, a ship has to be stable enough to stay the right way up even when it has to turn or in rough seas, and it has to stay afloat. A ship will only stay afloat if it is lighter than the weight of water it 'displaces' or pushes aside. In the nineteenth century, some ship owners overloaded their ships on purpose so they would sink and the owner could collect the insurance money. They were known as 'coffin ships' because many sailors drowned. As a result, Plimsoll marks were introduced as part of the Merchant Shipping Act of 1876 to prevent overloading. Plimsoll marks are named after Samuel Plimsoll, the MP for Derby, who worked hard to introduce the new law.

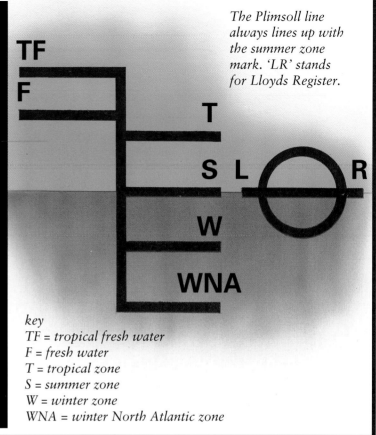

The Plimsoll line always lines up with the summer zone mark. 'LR' stands for Lloyds Register.

key
TF = tropical fresh water
F = fresh water
T = tropical zone
S = summer zone
W = winter zone
WNA = winter North Atlantic zone

LOADING SHIPS ON DIFFERENT SEAS

Great care must be taken when loading ships. Heavy cargoes should be put at the bottom and distributed evenly over the front, back and along the sides of the ship. This stops the ship tilting or even toppling over in the water. Plimsoll marks measure how much cargo a ship can safely carry in different water conditions. To set loading levels, the world is divided into zones. The tropical zone has better weather conditions than the winter North Atlantic zone so ships are allowed to load deeper. As fresh water contains no salt, it is lighter than sea water so ships lie deeper in fresh water.

Containers carry all sorts of cargoes, such as china, fruit and machinery. Containers can be loaded on and off lorries at the port.

Cargoes must be stowed securely so they don't move if the ship rolls. If they shift to one side they could stop the ship righting itself.

THE MARBLE GAME

Cut some equal sized pieces of modelling clay, but don't cut them too big.

Give each of your friends a piece to mould into a saucer-shaped boat. Float the boats in water. Which one holds the most marbles before it sinks?

You could then let each of your friends make his or her own shaped boat. (Make sure you give them each the same amount of modelling clay, again.)

Now test the boats for stability.

Make each of your boats as before but this time put a wooden building block in it. Then add another block and then another until the tower of bricks is so unstable that the boat topples to one side. Who has made the most stable boat? Is it the same as the one that held the greater load?

SELF-RIGHTING BOATS

A lifeboat is specially designed to cope with terrible weather conditions. The wheelhouse is watertight which means that air is trapped at the top of the boat. If the boat rolls on its side or turns upside-down, the light top and the heavy engines at the bottom pull the boat the right way up again. There are also airtight compartments in the hull so if the boat is punctured below the waterline it will still stay afloat. These compartments also give the lifeboat buoyancy and stability.

NAVIGATION

CAPTAIN COOK 1728–79
Captain Cook made three voyages of exploration. On the first he charted New Zealand. On the second he reached the furthest point south ever made and on the third he reached the furthest point north.

In huge oceans there are no landmarks to help guide ships. Navigation is the way ships at sea know their position and decide the direction they need to take to get to their destination. Modern ships have very advanced technology to help them find their way, but early navigators had lots of problems to overcome. To know exactly where they were going, they had to know the direction they were taking, their latitude and their longitude. Once people had learned how to find out these things and record them, they could chart new lands accurately and plan the safest routes for their sea journeys. Closer to land, lighthouses help a crew to work out a ship's position. Below, the great navigator Captain Cook is using a sextant to calculate his latitude.

CHARTING

Captain Cook was very skilled at making maps of the new lands he explored. On his first voyage, he spent six months accurately charting New Zealand. He didn't have a chronometer and had to observe the moon and use complex mathematical tables to work out his position along the coastline (see page 26).

Captain Cook's first voyage of exploration

HARRISON'S CHRONOMETER

In 1759, John Harrison won a competition to solve the problem of measuring longitude. He invented an accurate 'chronometer' or sea clock which only lost 2.7 seconds a day. With an accurate time-keeper, navigators could work out how far they had travelled east or west (see page 26). Captain Cook took a copy of the Harrison chronometer on his second and third voyages.

copies of the Harrison chronometer made by Larcum Kendall for Captain Cook

LATITUDE AND LONGITUDE

To find out where they were, people invented imaginary lines called longitude and latitude to divide up the Earth. If you know your longitude and latitude, you can pinpoint your position anywhere on Earth. Lines of longitude tell you how far east or west you are of the Prime Meridian – the line of longitude that runs through Greenwich in London. Lines of latitude tell you how many degrees north or south of the Equator you are. Centuries ago, people learned how to find their latitude, how far north or south they were, by observing the position of the sun or a star in the sky in relation to the horizon. But longitude remained a problem until the eighteenth century.

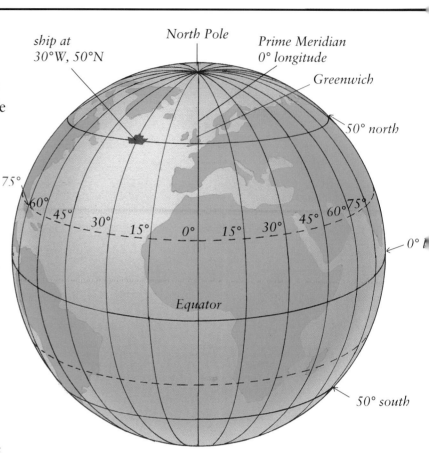

ship at 30°W, 50°N · North Pole · Prime Meridian 0° longitude · Greenwich · 50° north · 75° · 60° · 45° · 30° · 15° · 0° · 15° · 30° · 45° · 60° · 75° · 0° · Equator · 50° south

TIME ZONES AND NAVIGATION

Harrison's chronometer was important because it enabled navigators to work out their longitude accurately for the first time. They did this by comparing the time in Greenwich from their chronometer with midday wherever they were. The Earth is a sphere and so it spins through 360 degrees in every 24 hours. In an hour, the Earth moves through 360 ÷ 24 = 15 degrees. So, if it is 2pm in Greenwich and midday where the ship is, the ship must have travelled westwards by 2 × 15 = 30 degrees.

THE DEVELOPMENT OF NAVIGATION

The most important developments in navigation have overcome three basic problems – working out direction, calculating latitude and calculating longitude. In about 1000 BC, the Chinese discovered that lodestone points to the north, which led eventually to the invention of the compass. Since then, people have invented and improved methods of finding the way.

By fixing a piece of lodestone to a strand of straw and floating the straw in a bowl of water, people made a simple compass. Mediterranean people did this in the twelfth century.

Better compasses were developed later which showed all four directions. A magnetised needle was balanced on a spindle so it could rotate until it rested in a north/south direction. But magnetic compasses only point to magnetic north which is slightly different to true north (see glossary). Modern gyroscopic compasses always point to true north.

MAKE A MAGNETIC COMPASS

magnet | slice of cork | sticky tape

needle | magnetised needle

To make a magnetic compass, hold a steel needle firmly and stroke it from one end to the other with a magnet. Do this about 30 times. Always stroke in one direction. This magnetises the needle. Tape the needle to a thin slice of cork. Place this in a dish of water. It will come to rest pointing north/south. Cut a circle of card then cut out the middle to make a ring. Mark the ring with the points of the compass then place it on top of the dish. Rotate the ring of card until the compass needle lines up with 'N' for north. Your compass now shows north, south, east and west.

float the cork in the middle of a bowl of water

ring of card marked with compass points

cut the card about 4 cm wider than the dish

radar pulse transmitted

if there is another ship the radar pulse is reflected back

Radar pulses travel at the speed of light. It takes a few seconds for radar pulses to be transmitted around 360 degrees. Radar calculates the other ship's position, direction and speed from the echo it receives.

AVOIDING OTHER SHIPS

Today, there are many ships sailing along the world's busy sea routes. It is important not to bump into other vessels. This is done by using radar. The radar transmits pulses of energy one after another around 360 degrees. If an echo returns from another ship the radar calculates its position, direction and speed by measuring how long the echo takes to return. Ships can detect land using radar too.

CALCULATING LATITUDE

A cross staff was an early and imprecise way of measuring the position of the sun or stars in relation to the horizon to work out latitude.

The sextant was invented by Johann Mayer in 1757. This device can measure the precise angle of the sun or a star to the Earth.

CALCULATING LONGITUDE

Longitude was calculated using more and more accurate clocks until better devices were invented in this century. Radio signals from land stations and satellites can now be read by special computers to give the precise position of modern ships. They do this by comparing the time it takes for each signal to reach the ship.

POWERED SHIPS

THE CHARLOTTE DUNDAS
The first ship powered by steam was the Charlotte Dundas, *built in 1801. She had a single paddle-wheel at the stern.*

For thousands of years, people depended on the wind or their own muscle power to move their ships. Then, at the beginning of the nineteenth century, steam engines were adapted so that they could propel ships. As people's skill in making engines developed, so did their other technical skills like inventing new ways to propel ships and building ships of iron instead of wood. With new sources of power and new materials, larger and larger ships could be built until today we have supertankers which are up to 450 metres long! Below is the *Great Eastern*, a steamship designed by Isambard Kingdom Brunel. It was propelled by paddle-wheels and a propeller and it also used sails to save fuel.

PADDLES OR PROPELLERS?

The first steam engines turned a paddlewheel at the stern of the ship, or two paddlewheels at each side. But paddlewheels are not very efficient because most of the wheel is out of the water doing no work at all. Screw propellers, invented in the 1840s, are better because all the blades are work-ing in the water at the same time.

paddlewheel

In 1845, two steam-powered boats, one with paddlewheels and the other with a propeller, had a tug-of-war competition. The propeller-driven boat won!

type of propeller used until 1860s

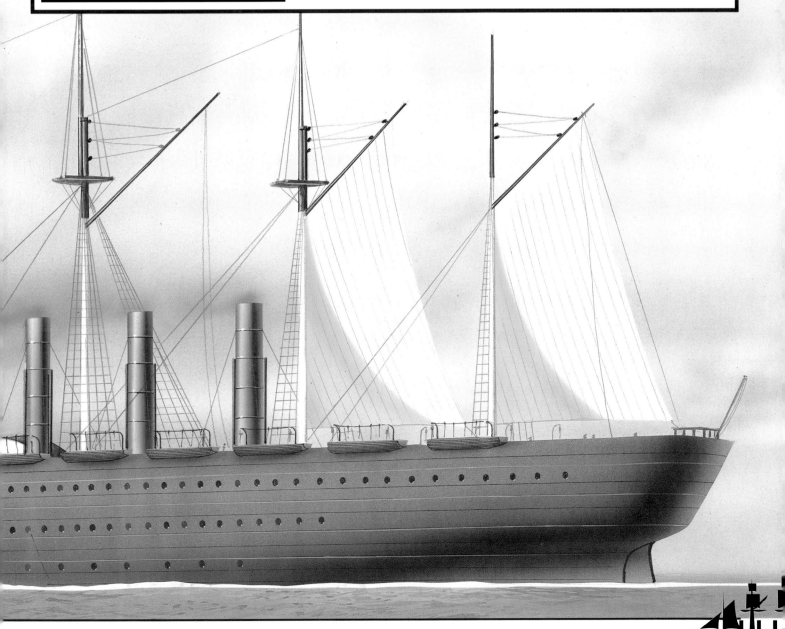

SIMPLE AND ADVANCED ENGINES

The first steam engines powered pistons attached to a crankshaft which then turned the paddlewheels or a propeller. The steam was produced by burning coal in a furnace which heated up water in a boiler. A turbine engine is more advanced than a piston engine because it uses steam or gas to turn windmill-like structures which drive the propeller directly through a gearbox. The blades of the turbine are set at an angle so they move round when the steam or gas hits them. These engines produce a great deal of power and are very reliable.

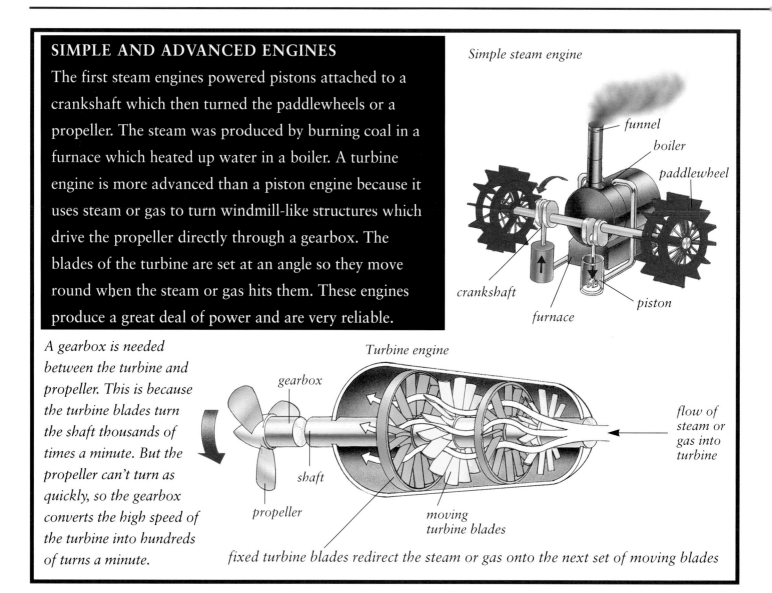

Simple steam engine

funnel
boiler
paddlewheel
crankshaft
furnace
piston

A gearbox is needed between the turbine and propeller. This is because the turbine blades turn the shaft thousands of times a minute. But the propeller can't turn as quickly, so the gearbox converts the high speed of the turbine into hundreds of turns a minute.

Turbine engine

gearbox
shaft
propeller
flow of steam or gas into turbine
moving turbine blades

fixed turbine blades redirect the steam or gas onto the next set of moving blades

THE DEVELOPMENT OF POWER

Since 1800, powered ships have developed quickly. Bigger, better engines have been invented to produce power more efficiently and move larger, faster ships.

EARLY STEAMSHIPS 1817
The first steamship to cross the English Channel was the Elise in 1817.

STEAM TURBINE 1884
The invention of turbine engines was a great advance because they can drive ships much faster than piston engines. At first, coal and then oil were burned to produce the steam. Steam turbines were used in great ocean-going liners like the Mauretania *and* Lusitania.

PISTON ENGINES

In these engines, pistons are moved up and down by steam, or by burning petrol or diesel. The pistons turn a crankshaft which in turn rotates a paddlewheel or propeller. Diesel engines are now the most common type of engine for ships. Each piston sits inside a cylinder. The more cylinders the ship has, the more power the engine can produce.

1. As the piston moves down in the cylinder, air is sucked in through the 'inlet valve'.

2. The inlet valve closes. The piston moves up which squeezes the air in the cylinder making it very hot.

3. Diesel oil is squirted into the cylinder by an 'injector'. The fuel catches alight and in the hot air it explodes and pushes the piston downwards.

4. The exhaust valve opens releasing waste gases.

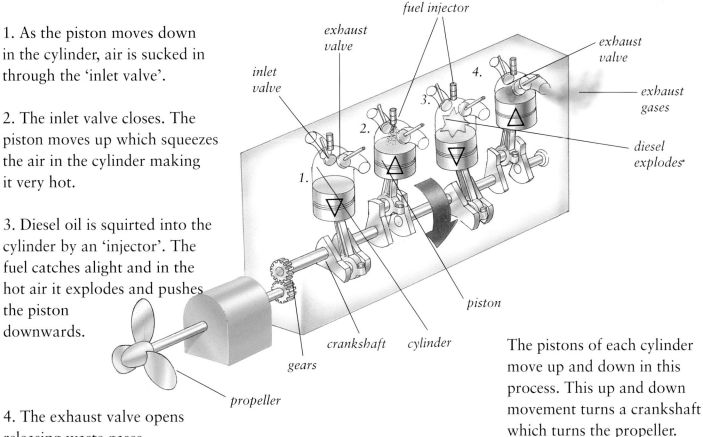

The pistons of each cylinder move up and down in this process. This up and down movement turns a crankshaft which turns the propeller.

DIESEL ENGINE 1897
Diesel engines are still common today in ships like ferries because they can produce a lot of power cheaply. Diesel engines are also used to generate electricity for ships like submarines and some modern warships.

GAS TURBINE SHIPS 1970s – TODAY
These ships burn fuels that produce hot expanding gases which then turn a turbine. They can travel at high speed but use a lot of fuel. Some warships and hydrofoils use this kind of engine – so do jet aircraft!

NUCLEAR POWER 1955 –TODAY
Nuclear power is mostly used in submarines and aircraft carriers. The nuclear reactor is used to produce steam which then turns a turbine. Nuclear power is very expensive, but it enables a ship to travel a long way without refuelling.

SUBMARINES

The first underwater vessel was built in 1620, but it wasn't until the beginning of the twentieth century when motors were invented that submarines really started to develop. The main reason why they needed to be developed was war. Because submarines cannot be seen from the surface, they can attack unsuspecting ships with torpedoes. The German U-boats of the First and Second World Wars destroyed many enemy ships, which encouraged other countries to design their own submarines. Submarines also developed so that people could explore the seabed for natural resources like oil or for shipwrecks like the *Titanic*. Submarines have to be watertight and have very strong hulls which are able to withstand great pressure. The deeper a submarine goes, the greater is the weight of water above it and the greater the pressure upon it.

UP PERISCOPE
A periscope is a metal tube up to 9 metres long. Inside are mirrors which allow the submarine's crew to see the surface of the sea while staying hidden underwater.

SONAR
Sonar are the submarine's main sensors. There are many types. Some can detect ships hundreds of kilometres away by sensing the noises made by their machinery. Other sonar transmit pulses of sound and listen for echoes reflected from other submarines.

TORPEDOES
Torpedoes are guided to their target by signals sent along thin wires which link the torpedo to the submarine.

EXHAUST MAST
At periscope depth underwater, the submarine can recharge its batteries using its diesel engines. The exhaust fumes flow out through one pipe and fresh air is drawn in through another.

CONTROL ROOM
The control room contains computers to help the crew find, track and attack ships and other submarines. There are also controls to manoeuvre the submarine.

PERISCOPES

RADAR MAST

FRONT HYDROPLANE

ACCOMMODATION
Sailors sleep on bunks. They have very small lockers for clothes and belongings.

BATTERIES
The batteries are found low down in the submarine. They power the electric motor.

AUXILIARY MACHINE ROOM
Special machinery here makes drinking water by removing salt from the sea water.

DIVING AND RISING

To make a submarine dive, valves (like large taps) in the outer hull are opened to let the air out and the sea water into the ballast tanks. The submarine becomes heavier and it begins to sink (1). The crew controls the amount of water in the tanks until the submarine neither sinks nor rises underwater. Its depth is then controlled by the hydroplanes. To surface, compressed air is blown into the ballast tanks which forces the water out through the valves (2). As the ballast tanks fill with air, the submarine becomes lighter and begins to rise (3).

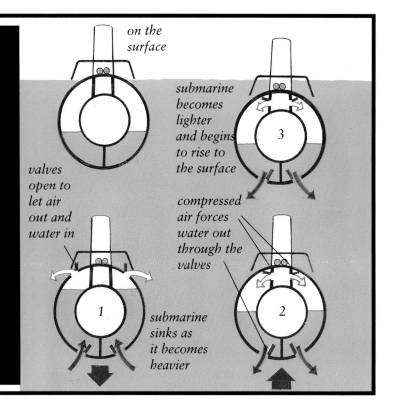

on the surface

submarine becomes lighter and begins to rise to the surface

valves open to let air out and water in

compressed air forces water out through the valves

submarine sinks as it becomes heavier

HYDROPLANES
When a submarine is underwater it can go up or down by tilting its hydroplanes. Depending on the way the hydroplane tilts, the water forced against it pushes the submarine up or down.

PROPELLER

RUDDER
Submarines have rudders to steer them just like ordinary ships.

ELECTRIC MOTOR
This very large motor drives the propeller.

MAIN DIESEL ENGINES
These are used to charge the batteries.

A CARTESIAN DIVER

Draw some water into a medicine dropper until it just floats in a glass of water. Put the dropper into a plastic lemonade bottle full of water. Screw on the top. Now squeeze the sides of the bottle – the dropper should sink. What happens to the water level inside the dropper? Stop squeezing the bottle and the dropper should rise again. Squeezing the bottle increases the pressure on the water inside which is then forced into the dropper, making it heavier so it sinks. Releasing the bottle reduces the pressure so the extra water inside the dropper is sucked out and it floats again.

water level

glass of water

screw the top on tightly

water level

water level rises when the bottle is squeezed

THE MIR SUBMERSIBLE

Submersibles are small submarines used to explore the sea. Some have specially designed hulls which can withstand massive pressure. In 1991, two submersibles were used to film the wreck of the *Titanic*, the luxury liner that sank on its maiden voyage in 1912. It took the Mirs three hours to make the 4 km trip to the seabed where the *Titanic* lies.

DIVING SUITS

This extraordinary diving suit has been specially designed for working in deep water. The deeper you go, the greater the pressure of the water and normal diving suits cannot protect the diver from being crushed. This suit can withstand great pressure but also has special joints so that the person inside can move easily. Vital work such as repairing oil rigs or underwater pipelines can then be carried out.

The first submarine used in war was the Turtle, *built by David Bushnell in 1776. It was made of wood so it could not withstand the pressure of very deep water. It carried tanks which filled with water to make it sink just under the surface.*

1776 (American War of Independence)

In the mid-nineteenth century, hand and then steam power were used in 'David' submarines. The 'David' was the first submarine to sink an enemy ship in the American Civil War, but the explosion also sank the submarine!

1861–65 (American Civil War)

THE DEVELOPMENT OF THE SUBMARINE

Early submarines, like the *Turtle*, had no engines and were driven by muscle power, but true submarines were not possible until electric motors powered by batteries were invented. At first, petrol and diesel engines generated electricity to charge the batteries. After the Second World War, nuclear power was developed to drive submarines and nuclear missiles were introduced as a new kind of weapon.

A WORKING MODEL SUBMARINE

You can make a working model of a craft that will sink and then rise like a submarine from a plastic drinks bottle. You can operate it with some plastic tubing or a rubber hose – a 1.5 metre length is suitable. First cut two holes in the bottle towards the base.

Load the bottle with pebbles or marbles and put it into a bucket of water so that it is upright on its base. Make sure the top is screwed on tightly.

Now insert your tubing through one of the holes and blow into it.

The bottle should rise because the air you are blowing into the bottle will force the water out of the bottle and make it light enough to float. If the bottle is too heavy, remove some of the pebbles or marbles.

To make your submarine sink again, simply unscrew the bottle top to let the air escape.

By 1900, petrol engines were used to power American 'Holland' submarines.

1890s – 1900

Diesel engines are used today in some submarines. But diesel engines create exhaust fumes, so the submarine has to rise almost to the surface so it can release the fumes through a pipe and take in fresh air.

1897 – today

In nuclear submarines, reactors make steam which drives turbines. These submarines could stay underwater for several years, but the crew has to surface for fresh air and food supplies. Underwater, the crew breathe air which is purified by special equipment.

1955 – today

HYDROFOIL AND HOVERCRAFT

THE FIRST HYDROFOIL
The first hydrofoil to be tested successfully was built by Enrico Forlanini in Italy in 1906. The propellers for this hydrofoil were in the air rather than underwater.

Most ships have to force their way through the water to move forward which limits their speed. The deeper the ship's hull sits in the water, the more water it has to push out of the way when it is moving. But hydrofoils and hovercraft are specially designed to ride above the water which makes them faster than ordinary ships. A hydrofoil has 'wings' built underneath which lift the hull up out of the water when it reaches a certain speed. A hydrofoil is known as a 'semi-submersible' ship because only the foils are in the water when it is at cruising speed. Hovercraft are not really ships at all because they don't even touch the water! They 'fly' on a cushion of air just above the surface. They can travel over land too.

THE HYDROFOIL
Because the hull of a hydrofoil lifts out of the water, there is less friction between the ship and the water and so it can travel at speeds of up to 55 knots. In rough seas the foils just cut straight through the waves, and flaps on the foils can be adjusted to keep the ship stable. As the hydrofoil slows down, the hull sinks back into the water like a normal ship.

two different designs of hydrofoil

HYDRODYNAMICS

The *shape* of the foil lifts the boat out of the water. As the boat picks up speed, water is forced over the curved surface of the foil faster than along the flat surface. So there is more pressure beneath which pushes the foil upwards.

flow of water is faster over the top of the foil

direction of travel

foil

lift

more pressure underneath the foil causes lift

strut can be turned to steer the ship

foils

flaps operated by computer help raise the ship out of the water and keep it stable

UP SHE GOES

You can simulate how the 'wings' on a hydrofoil work.

Fold a sheet of A4 paper in half.

Curve and glue the top half to the bottom half.

Make a hole through both sheets. Push a length of drinking straw through the hole.

Thread a piece of cotton through the straw. Ask a friend to blow on the wing.

The wing will rise in the air. What do they think will happen if they blow from the other side?

CATAMARAN

Catamarans have two narrow hulls running along their length which are joined by the main part of the ship. This design spreads the weight of the ship over a large area. Because the hulls are narrow, they displace or push aside less water than an ordinary ship with the same capacity. This reduces the drag of the water which means catamarans can travel very quickly. The 'wave-piercing' catamaran on the right has a maximum speed of 42 knots and a cruising speed of 35 knots. It is 74 metres long – just a little longer than a jumbo jet – and 26 metres wide. Its engines are linked directly to water jets which propel the catamaran. Other water jets control steering and reversing. Because of the way they spread their weight, catamarans are very stable and they can be built much larger than hydrofoils. They can carry up to 80 cars as well as passengers. Huge new catamarans, the size of a soccer pitch, are now being designed which will be able to carry lorries too (below).

Catamarans like the one below provide ferry services in Britain, Scandinavia, Australia and South America.

In June 1990, a catamaran called the Hoverspeed Great Britain *won the Hales 'Blue Riband' Trophy for the fastest crossing of the Atlantic Ocean. It took three days, seven hours and 54 minutes at an average speed of 36.6 knots.*

A CUSHION OF AIR

Hovercraft fly about 3 metres above the water. Powerful gas turbine engines turn enormous fans that push air downwards underneath the craft. The pressure of this air is slightly higher than the surrounding air so the hovercraft lifts up. The skirt around the craft traps the air and keeps the pressure under the hovercraft higher than it is outside. The skirt is flexible and acts like a shock absorber so the craft can move smoothly. The engines also turn propellers which push the hovercraft forward and steer it. Hovercraft can travel at speeds of up to 70 knots. They are large enough to carry cars, which must be arranged carefully on the car deck to distribute their weight evenly.

hovercraft at rest

rudder *propellers*

rubber skirt

hovercraft in motion

cushion of air

MAKE A HOVERCRAFT

You can make a hovercraft with a polystyrene food tray and a yoghurt pot. Draw round the base of the yoghurt pot to mark a circle at the centre of the food tray. Cut this out. Cut the base off the yoghurt pot and jam the pot into the hole in the food tray. Using a hairdryer, blow air through the yoghurt pot. The friction between tray and tabletop is reduced by the pressure of the air forced under the tray, so it lifts up and 'floats'.

cut off base of yoghurt pot

cut hole in polystyrene tray

blow air in top

tray lifts on a cushion of air

Make two holes through the skirt at one end of the hovercraft. Air escaping through the holes will push the craft in the opposite direction.

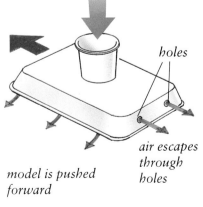

holes

air escapes through holes

model is pushed forward

SPORTING CRAFT

Ever since people first worked out how to travel on water they have wanted to go faster and further than others. For centuries there have been races in ships and boats powered by oars or the wind. Nowadays, people have more leisure time and money so they can enjoy water sports. This has led to many new kinds of sports being developed for competition and fun. New materials, designs, types of propulsion and fuels have led to a wide variety of sporting craft.

ROWING AND PADDLING

Rowing, canoeing and kayaking are very popular sports. In rowing, a new oar shape was introduced in 1992 called a 'cleaver'. The blade has a larger surface area than the traditional design so it moves more water, but it is shorter so it has less leverage on the water (see page 13). In kayak racing, a newly designed paddle with a curved edge can increase the competitor's speed, saving three seconds over 1,000 metres.

POWER BOATS

Racing power boats are designed to compete at high speeds. Some have jet engines like those used in jet aeroplanes – others use powerful petrol or diesel engines. The hulls are designed so that, as the boats speed up, they skim over the waves, reducing the drag of the water so they can go even faster. Jetskis also use powerful engines to suck water through a device called an impeller. This forces water at high speed through a nozzle at the back of the ski to push it along.

SAILING

To go as fast as possible, sailors want to avoid two problems which reduce their speed. The first is being pushed sideways by the wind. A centreboard or a keel helps to stop this. The second problem is being pushed too far over by the wind on the sail. Lightweight masts and sails made of new carbon fibre materials make the top of a boat lighter so it is easier for the centreboard or keel to counterbalance the wind.

TRIMARANS AND CATAMARANS

Trimarans (with three hulls) and catamarans (with two hulls) make very fast racing yachts. This is because there is less water drag on their long narrow hulls compared with ordinary yachts. They are also very stable and don't lean or 'heel' over too much which helps them go faster. Lots of power boats now use a catamaran design too.

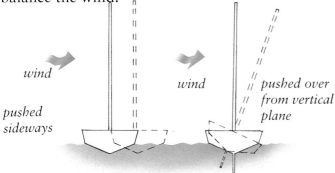

wind

pushed sideways

wind

pushed over from vertical plane

WINDSURFING

Windsurfers are made of fibreglass and nylon, which are cheap enough for lots of people to afford, so windsurfing is very popular. Windsurfers also have the advantage of being portable, simple to put together and easy to sail – after a bit of practice! Windsurfers come in all shapes and sizes – some are designed for speed and others for tricks and jumps.

WINGED KEEL

Some large racing yachts now have winged keels. This means the weight of the keel is lower in the water. The lower the weight, the better the keel counterbalances the force of the wind on the sails. This keeps the yacht more upright and means the sails can 'catch' more of the wind.

SHIPS OF THE FUTURE

The designs of ships change either because people need the ship to do new or different things or because new inventions have produced a technological advance. People in the future will come up with new designs for hulls, new materials to build with, new sources of power and better engines that won't damage the environment.

SPECIAL NEEDS

Smuggling and piracy are a big problem. In the future, police forces might use ships like this one (above) to stop crime at sea. This ship cannot be detected easily because it has a specially designed shape which reduces radar echoes and it uses a remarkable material which absorbs radar pulses. It can locate other ships at night, while staying hidden itself, by using infra-red heat sensors or information sent to it by satellite. It also uses sonar to listen to the noises made by other ships or submarines. It can travel at speeds of 45 knots even in rough seas and can chase, stop or destroy other ships with its guns, missiles or directed energy weapons (high-powered lasers).

FUEL ECONOMY

Today, a cargo ship produces the same amount of exhaust fumes as 10,000 cars. New technology is now developing which uses 'sails' shaped like aircraft wings turned on end. The force that lifts an aircraft off the ground can be used to push the ship along. Computers set the 'sails' at the best angle to the wind. This way, ships will be able to save fuel and protect the environment.

POWER AND PROPULSION

As fuels like coal and oil become scarce and pollution increases, people will develop new ways of powering ships. In the future they might use 'magneto-hydrodynamic' systems that use strong magnetic fields to force sea water through tubes which act like water jets. Or they might use energy from the sun to split water into hydrogen and oxygen. The hydrogen is then burned in special engines and the only exhaust is water.

MATERIALS

Catamarans (see page 38) and trimarans are cleverly designed because they spread the weight of a large ship over two or three slim hulls. In the future, ultra-strong and light materials might be developed that will make it possible to build enormous liner-type multi-hulled ships which can carry passengers across the Atlantic Ocean.

GLOSSARY

AIR RESISTANCE The drag of air on objects moving through it.

BOAT Small, open craft without any deck.

BOW The front end of a ship.

BUOYANCY The ability of a ship to stay afloat.

CARVEL PLANKING Where the external planks of a hull are fixed edge to edge with each other.

CAULKING A method of filling gaps between a ship's planking using oakum and melted pitch to make the hull watertight.

CENTRE LINE An imaginary line running down the middle of the ship from the bow to the stern.

CENTREBOARD A board in the bottom of a dinghy which acts like a keel. The board can be raised and lowered.

CLINKER PLANKING Where the external planks of a hull overlap the ones below.

DISPLACED WATER Water that is pushed out of the way by an object that is put in it, such as a ship. If the weight of the water pushed aside is heavier than the object, then the object will float.

GYROSCOPIC COMPASS A compass that uses a gyroscope. A gyroscope is a device which always spins on the same axis and this axis can be set to point to true north. A gyroscopic compass is more accurate than a magnetic compass because it is not affected by the Earth's magnetic field or any magnetism produced by the metal hull of the ship.

HULL The outer body of a ship.

HYDRODYNAMICS The effects and forces produced by and on water when objects are moving through it.

HYDROPLANE A fin on a submarine which tilts up or down. This makes the submarine move up or down when travelling underwater.

KNOTS The way of measuring speed at sea – 1 knot equals 1.85 km per hour.

LATITUDE A way of finding out how far north or south of the Equator you are. The Equator is 0° latitude. Other lines of latitude run parallel to the Equator up to 90° at the North and South Poles. By working out your longitude and latitude, you can pinpoint your exact position anywhere on Earth.

LONGITUDE A way of finding out how far east or west of the Prime Meridian you are. Lines of longitude divide the Earth like the segments of an orange – they are further apart at the Equator and meet at the Poles. By working out your longitude and latitude, you can pinpoint your exact position anywhere on Earth.

MAGNETIC NORTH The Earth's core contains a huge amount of metal which creates an enormous magnetic field over the planet. One end of this magnetic field is very close to but not exactly the same as true north. Magnetic compasses point to the northernmost part of this magnetic field and not to true north. Navigators have to consider this when they are calculating their position using a magnetic compass.

MULTI-HULLED SHIPS Ships like catamarans or trimarans which have more than one hull. The hulls are narrower than normal ships so there is less water drag on multi-hulled craft.

OAKUM Fibres from untwisted ropes. This material was forced into the gaps between planks in ships' hulls and sealed with pitch to make the hulls watertight.

PITCH A sticky, black substance made from tar or wood. It is liquid when hot and goes hard when cold, and it is waterproof.

PLIMSOLL LINE A line painted on the outside of a ship's hull which marks where the water level should be when the ship is loaded with cargo in certain sea conditions or areas.

PRIME MERIDIAN The line of longitude that passes through the Royal Observatory in Greenwich, London. It is 0° longitude.

RADAR An instrument that uses radio waves to measure the distance to an object and its speed and direction.

REEFING Reducing the size of a sail. This is done in strong winds to prevent the ship from being blown over.

RUDDER A flat plate which is hinged to the stern of a ship and used to steer the ship.

SEAWORTHINESS A fit state to be at sea. Ships have to be stable and buoyant to be seaworthy.

SHIP Generally an ocean-going vessel with a deck.

SONAR A device that detects the location and what an object is underwater by using sound waves.

STABILITY A stable ship is able to stay the right way up, even in rough seas.

STEAM TURBINE An engine in which steam generated in a separate boiler is used to drive a set of blades called a turbine. The turbine rotates thousands of times a minute and a gearbox then transfers this power directly to the propeller.

STERN The back part of a ship.

TRUE NORTH The northernmost part of the Earth, also known as the North Pole. The lines of latitude and longitude north of the Equator meet here. This is one end of the Earth's axis and the South Pole is at the other end. The Earth spins around this north-south axis.

U-BOAT German submarine of the First and Second World Wars. U-boat is short for *Unterseeboot* or 'undersea boat'.

INDEX